Career Planning
for
High School
Students

From a Christian Perspective

ADRIAN GONZALEZ

WESTBOW
PRESS®
A DIVISION OF THOMAS NELSON
& ZONDERVAN

WestBow Press books may be ordered through booksellers or by contacting:

WestBow Press
A Division of Thomas Nelson & Zondervan
1663 Liberty Drive
Bloomington, IN 47403
www.westbowpress.com
1 (866) 928-1240

Scripture taken from the King James Version of the Bible.

Scripture quotations are from the ESV® Bible (The Holy Bible, English Standard Version®), copyright © 2001 by Crossway, a publishing ministry of Good News Publishers. Used by permission. All rights reserved.

Scripture taken from the New King James Version®. Copyright © 1982 by Thomas Nelson. Used by permission. All rights reserved.

Scripture quotations taken from the New American Standard Bible® (NASB), Copyright © 1960, 1962, 1963, 1968, 1971, 1972, 1973, 1975, 1977, 1995 by The Lockman Foundation Used by permission.

ISBN: 978-1-9736-1181-3 (sc)
ISBN: 978-1-9736-1180-6 (e)

Library of Congress Control Number: 2017919388

Print information available on the last page.

WestBow Press rev. date: 2/26/2018

Contents

Acknowledgements vi

Introduction vii

The Gospel Message viii

The Foundation of Biblical Career Planning x

Chapter 1: Become an active member of the Church 1

Chapter 2: Learn to Submit to Authority 5

Chapter 3: Learn to Receive Discipline and Correction with Humility 17

**Chapter 4: Investor Approach to Career Discovery and Planning
(Adopting an investor approach to God's given gift)** 21

What are the leading industries where I live? (Step 1) 24

Which of these leading industries am I interested in? (Step 2) 31

Who are the leading employers in the industry I have chosen? (Step 3) 40

What jobs do these top employers/market leaders need to fill? (Step 4) 44

To which of these jobs can I contribute the most? (Step 5) 48

Conclusion 59

The Ultimate Career Goal 60

Acknowledgements

I want to thank my editor, Lee Ann, from FirstEditing.com, for helping me in bringing this manuscript to completion. Without her guidance, dedication, and knowledge, this book wouldn't have been possible.

Introduction

The decisions involved in choosing a career can be overwhelming. You wish for God to just show up and literally tell you what it is He wants you to do. If this is your case, how would you feel if someone told you that what you are asking is possible? The truth is, the Bible reveals the heart and mind of God for all aspects of living, including your professional career. When you want to know what something is useful for, you read the manufacturer's instructions and you will find the intended use. In this same manner, God, your Creator, is the only one who really knows for what specific purpose you were designed, and the instructions are found in the Bible. The only condition, though, is that to find out, you must become a Christian. Therefore, if you are interested in finding God's will for you, flip the page and read the following message. Your response to the Gospel message will determine if career planning from a biblical perspective is for you.

The Gospel Message

The Bible says that we all have sinned against God: "For all have sinned, and come short of the glory of God" (Romans 3:23 King James Version). It doesn't matter how many good deeds we have done, we don't measure up to God's standard of right and wrong. The Bible also says that there is a punishment for our sins: "For the wages of sin is death" (Romans 6:23). We are all going to die one day physically, but this physical death is not the end. The Bible talks about a second death in the book of Revelation: "And death and hell were cast into the lake of fire. This is the second death" (Revelation 20:14-15). In this verse, the lake of fire is what is known as the second death. Those who end up in this place will be tormented forever and ever as punishment for their sins: "And the devil that deceived them was cast into the lake of fire and brimstone, where the beast and the false prophet are, and shall be tormented day and night for ever and ever" (Revelation 20:10).

Further down in Revelation, you can find the list of people who are going to this lake of fire: "But the fearful, and unbelieving, and the abominable, and murderers, and whoremongers, and sorcerers, and idolaters, and all liars, shall have their part in the lake which burneth with fire and brimstone: which is the second death" (Revelation 21:8). Perhaps you are not a murderer or sorcerer; but what about a liar? Have you ever told at least one lie in your life? According to the Bible, all liars are heading to the lake of fire and brimstone: "As it is written, there is none righteous, no, not one" (Romans 3:10). A righteous man or woman is someone who always does what is right before God. Do you always do the right thing? If you don't, then you'd better listen to this important message: God loves you, and doesn't want you to die and suffer in Hell for an eternity. However, you must understand too that He must punish sin. God is just and fair. If He allowed ours sins to go unpunished, He would not be a righteous God.

Let's say, for example, that a thief robbed your house and in the attempt, also killed your dad and mom. Would the judge be a fair judge if he said to this thief "Well... since you only killed two people, I'll let you go home if you promise not to do it again"? Would that be justice? Of course not. But how can God punish sin and at the same time love us? The answer is found on the cross. In it, God found a substitute to take the punishment for our sins. A substitute is someone or something that takes the place of someone or something else, and Christ took our place on the cross. "But God commendeth his love toward us, in that, while we were yet sinners, Christ died for us" (Romans 5:8). When Jesus was on the cross, it was as if He had done every sin that you have ever done, even though He lived a sinless life.

When Jesus died for our sins, he took upon himself the punishment for our past, present, and future sins. However, not everybody is going to be automatically saved. There is one thing we must do. "And brought them out, and said, Sirs, what must I do to be saved? And they said, believe on the Lord Jesus Christ, and thou shalt be saved, and thy house" (Acts 16:30). What does this verse say that we must do to be saved? Believe in Jesus. Here is why: "For God so loved the world, that he gave his only begotten Son, that whosoever believeth in him should not perish, but have everlasting life" (John 3:16). Does this verse say that you must go to church, stop sinning, and live a perfect life? No, that is not what it says. This verse clearly states that salvation from hell is not by our good deeds and it is not by obeying God's commandants (if that was even humanly possible). It is by believing in

Christ, by faith in Christ, trusting Jesus as your savior. Believing in Jesus is transferring your trust and dependence from your good deeds and depositing it in God's grace.

Now, let's go back to Romans 6:23 and read the rest of the verse we started with. "For the wages of sin is death; but the gift of God is eternal life through Jesus Christ our Lord" (Romans 6:23). Grace is receiving a gift that we don't pay for; in this case, it is the gift of everlasting life in God's presence. "For by grace are ye saved through faith; and that not of yourselves: it is the gift of God: Not of works, lest any man should boast" (Ephesians 2:8-9). It is important that you understand this because probably all religions in the worlds—Catholics, Muslims, Jehovah's Witness, and Mormons—will tell you that to be saved, you must obey a list of manmade commandments and perform certain rituals/personal sacrifices, or even obey the commandments of the Law.

Therefore, let's review the Gospel message once again to make sure you understand it. How are we saved? By grace. What is grace? A gift from God we don't deserve. Who pays for the gift? Jesus. How did Jesus pay for that gift? By dying on the cross. How much do we have to pay for the gift of everlasting life? Nothing. The Bible says that if you believe in Jesus you will have everlasting life, end of discussion. "These things I have written unto you that believe in the name of the Son of God; that ye may know that ye have eternal life, and that ye may believe on the name of the Son of God" (1 John 5:13). "He that believeth on the Son hath everlasting life: and he that believeth not the Son shalt not see life; but the wrath of God abideth on him" (John 3:36).

In summary, we are all sinners that deserve death. Christ died for our sins and rose again. Believing in Him is what saves us from the second death. The question to you now is: Do you believe that you are a sinner? Do believe that you deserve to go to hell because of your sins? Do you believe that Jesus died for your sins and that He was buried and rose again? If the answer to all these questions is yes, then just tell God right now that is what you believe. The Bible says that: "For whosoever shall call upon the name of the Lord shall be saved" (Romans 10:13). Here is how you can call on the name of the Lord for salvation:

> "Dear Jesus, I believe that I am a sinner, but I believe you died for my sins and rose again. Please save me, and give me everlasting life. I am only trusting you for my salvation. Amen."

The Bible says that "… if thou shalt confess with thy mouth the Lord Jesus, and shalt believe in thine heart that God hath raised him from the dead, thou shalt be saved. For with the heart man believeth unto righteousness; and with the mouth confession is made unto salvation" (Romans 10:9-10).

The Foundation of Biblical Career Planning

The foundation of biblical career planning is found in Exodus 31:1-6.

The Lord said to Moses:

> See, I have called by name Bezalel the son of Uri, son of Hur, of the tribe of Judah, and I have filled him with the Spirit of God, with ability and intelligence, with knowledge and all craftsmanship, to devise artistic designs, to work in gold, silver, and bronze, in cutting stones for setting, and in carving wood, to work in every craft. And behold, I have appointed with him Oholiab, the son of Ahisamach, of the tribe of Dan. And I have given to all able men ability, that they may make all that I have commanded you (Exodus 31:1-6 English Standard Version).

In this passage, we witness God giving specific talents (ability, intelligence, and knowledge of craftsmanship) to these two individuals for building the tabernacle. In this tabernacle, the people of Israel will sacrifice a lamb once a year for the forgiveness of their sins and in this way, get closer with God to have a relationship with Him. God is holy, and He requires the same holiness from whosoever stands in his presence to have a relationship with Him.

The Israelites knew that the only way for a sinful man or women to approach a holy God was to be cleansed by the blood of an *innocent lamb*, as it was written in their law: "And almost all things are by the law purged with blood; and without shedding of blood is no remission" (Hebrews 9:22). Once the lamb was chosen, the person who wanted his or her sin to be forgiven would lay his hand on it: "And he shall put his hand upon the head of the burnt offering; and it shall be accepted to make atonement for him" (Leviticus 1:4). By laying his hands on the animal, the person's sins were transferred to the lamb. Then, the high priest would slaughter the lamb for the atonement of that individual's sins. Blood is what made the atonement possible: "For the life of the flesh is in the blood: and I have given it to you upon the altar to make an atonement for your souls for it is the blood that maketh an atonement for the soul" (Leviticus 17:11).

Simply put, once sins were transferred to the lamb, the lamb would pay the consequences of the wrongdoings of that person (the definition of atonement). The only problem with this atonement was that it did not remove sin permanently; therefore, God had to offer his only Son, Jesus Christ, as the ultimate, one-time sacrifice to satisfy God's wrath and fully atone for sin forever: "By the which will we are sanctified through the offering of the body of Jesus Christ once for all" (Hebrews 10:10).

Jesus is the Lamb of God that was led to slaughter and was pierced for our sins. His blood was shed on the cross of Calvary for the redemptions of our sins: "Forasmuch as ye know that ye were not redeemed with corruptible things, as silver and gold, from your vain conversation received by tradition from your fathers; But with the precious blood of Christ, as of a lamb without blemish and without spot" (1 Peter 1:18-19). Just as Isaiah prophesied some 700 years before Jesus' coming: "Surely he hath borne our griefs, and carried our sorrows: yet we did esteem him stricken, smitten of God, and afflicted. But he was wounded for our transgressions, he was bruised for our iniquities: the chastisement of our peace was upon him; and with his stripes we are healed. All we like sheep have gone astray; we have turned every one to his own way; and the LORD hath laid on him the iniquity of us all. He was oppressed, and he was afflicted, yet he opened not his mouth: he is brought as a lamb to the slaughter, and as a sheep before her shearers is dumb, so he openeth not his mouth" (Isaiah 53:4-7).

There is nothing we can do on our own effort to escape the punishment for our sins unless we find someone who has never sinned to take our place. That someone is Jesus. Because He is God, He is without sin, and because He is human, like us, He can take the punishment of death. Jesus qualifies to take our place, as the Scripture says: "For he hath made him to be sin for us, who knew no sin; that we might be made the righteousness of God in him" (2 Corinthians 5:21). When we trust Jesus Christ as our Savior, God the Father only sees Jesus's righteousness when He looks at us. Through Jesus we become holy in God's sight. "And ye know that he was manifested to take away our sins; and in him is no sin" (1 John 3:5).

Consider this now; if God gave Bezalel and Oholiab's talents for completing the tabernacle so that sinful people could have a temporary relationship with Him, would He not pour much more talents on His people for the gospel mission so that at last sinners could have a relationship with Him forever?

Career planning cannot begin unless you understand this truth. This why it was presented to you at the beginning. But now that you have a relationship with God and understand His mission, we want to tell you that God will also bestow talents on you, just as He did to Bezalel and Oholiab, if you meet the following four prerequisites, which constitute the foundation of biblical career planning.

- ✓ Become an active member of the Church
- ✓ Learn to submit to authority
- ✓ Learn to receive discipline and correction with humility
- ✓ Adopt an investor approach to God's given gift (investor approach to career discovery and planning)

Once the final prerequisite is met, you are going to be able to identify God's given talent for you. How can we ascertain this with 100 percent accuracy? Well... these prerequisites follow the same pattern of Bezalel to Oholiab, under the same conditions, to guarantee the same end results (God-given career gift). Let's get started.

Become an active member of the Church

In the Foundation of Biblical Career Planning section, you learned that God always gives talents to man with a specific mission in mind. In the same manner, God gave talent to Bezalel and Oholiab to complete the tabernacle so that sinners could have a relationship with Him. You are going to receive talents if you purpose in your heart to use them for the Gospel so sinners can have a relationship with God. But, how do you know this for a fact? The answer is easy; God's mission is always expressed in His commandments. Here is the commandment Bezalel and Oholiab received:

"And in the hearts of all that are wise hearted I have put wisdom, that they may make all that I have commanded thee; The tabernacle of the congregation, and the ark of the testimony, and the mercy seat that is thereupon, and all the furniture of the tabernacle." (Exodus 31:6-7) This was so the tabernacle could be completed, sacrifices performed, and people were able to come closer to God (at least from time to time, until the promise of the Savior was fulfilled).

Now here is the commandment you have received:

"Go ye therefore, and teach all nations, baptizing them in the name of the Father, and of the Son, and of the Holy Ghost: Teaching them to observe all things whatsoever I have commanded you: and, lo, I am with you always, even unto the end of the world. Amen" (Matthew 28:19). This is so the sinner would be able to have a relationship with God forever.

But, how do I do that? you may ask. Do I become a missionary or a pastor? The answer is no. The easiest way to obey this commandment is to become an active member of your church.

The objective of the local church is to impact communities with the Gospel. Every effort is directed at winning souls and making disciples, so when you actively get involved in their activities, you are obeying this commandant.

Now, why did God place becoming an active member of the Church as the first prerequisite? If you look as this passage, the first thing you realize is that Bezalel and Oholiab were not called randomly from the streets; they were set apart for the job from the congregation they were part of. "I have called by name Bezalel the son of Uri, son of Hur, of the tribe of Judah and I have appointed with him Oholiab, the son of Ahisamach, of the tribe of Dan" (Exodus 31:1-6 ESV). What is the logic behind this? you may ask. Well… think of God as an employer looking for an employee for a very important task. Would He pick someone from the street or would He pick someone in-house who has shown faithfulness and commitment? The choice is easy, wouldn't you think? However, this is not the only reason becoming an active member of the Church is the first prerequisite to receive a talent from God.

Let's take a closer look at Exodus 31:3 (KJV): "I have filled him with the Spirit of God, in wisdom, and in understanding, and in knowledge, in all manner of workmanship." Notice in this verse how the filling of the Holy Spirit comes first, then the list of gifts. You received the Holy Spirit when you trusted Jesus Christ as your Savior, but you are filled with the Spirit when your life is controlled by It through prayer and regular study of the Bible.

When you pray, you talk to God. When you study the Bible, God speaks to you. And when you obey what God is telling you to do, the filling of the Spirit takes place. Simply put, you are filled with the Holy Spirit when you allow the Holy Spirit to get rid of sin in your life to become more like Jesus. Therefore, have an intimate relationship with your Father in Heaven, and He will give you, through His Holy Spirit, the special abilities you need to complete His mission. The Holy Spirit creates the communication channel whereby the gifts are transferred from God to you.

Obviously, they are not going to be encouraged to seek God in the public school system. You can only receive this encouragement if you actively attend church, during Sunday school, disciplining classes, and listening to good preaching. Hence, the importance of becoming an active member of the Church.

In summary, you can safely say that when you become involve in your local church, you are obeying God's commandment, fulling God's mission, and your specific career talents will be manifested supernaturally as you progress through the prerequisites ahead, beginning with submitting to authority, coming next. In the meantime, complete the following activity.

Prerequisite 1 Activity

Becoming an active member of the church is the first qualification to receiving God-given talents. Both Bezalel and Oholiab had a specific purpose within their local congregation, and so do you. In the space below, write the name of your local church. If you don't have one, this is the time to find one and officially become a member.

Notes

Notes

Learn to Submit to Authority

Let's begin this section with a quick review of the first prerequisite. The following bullet points will help you remember that:

- God's given career gifts come to fulfill God's mission;
- God's mission is expressed in His commandments;
- It is the local church's duty to carry out God's mission;
- When you become an active member of your church, you are obeying God's commandment, fulfilling His mission, and your specific career gift is manifested supernaturally.

Simple, right? Now, looking at this same passage, to whom were the details of God's mission given to? To Moses. "And the LORD spake unto Moses" (Exodus 31:1).

Also, to whom were the specific instructions on how the tabernacle needed to be built given to? To Moses, again. "And in the hearts of all that are wise hearted I have put wisdom, that they may make all that I have commanded thee" (Exodus 31:6). And who was Moses? The leader, the boss, the person in authority.

The specifics of God's mission will always be shown to a leader first, just as the mission and goals of your future employer are going to be given to the business's management you are going to be working for one day. Therefore, the second prerequisite to receive God's given career gifts is that you learn to be subject to authority. To submit to authorities is not a natural desire, feeling, or emotion. On the contrary, it is a decision to obey God.

For this prerequisite, the Bible instructs the following: "Put them in mind to be subject to principalities and powers, to obey magistrates, to be ready to every good work" (Titus 3:1).

In the same manner that the directions to build the tabernacle were given to Moses (authority figure) and then passed on to Oholiab and Bezalel (you), the directions on how your career gift is going to fulfill a need in your local church and in your secular job will be given to an authority figure. Therefore, it is your responsibility to be subject to their authority: "Obey them that have the rule over you, and submit yourselves: for they watch for your souls, as they that must give account, that they may do it with joy, and not with grief: for that is unprofitable for you" (Hebrews 13:17 NKJV).

The biblical principle of submitting to authority not only applies to your function within the Church and secular work, but to all other areas of your life as well. As stated in Romans 13, all institutions, whether a government, a business, or the family, serve a specific purpose within God's established order. For each intended purpose, certain individuals are placed in charge to be responsible for enforcing order and the rules/procedures that will make the organization succeed. As a Christian, it is critical for your career development that you learn to be subject to all in position of authority (father, mother, teachers, bosses, and government authorities), and you do so whether you agree or disagree with their decisions. They might not have set good examples to follow at times, and/or have make mistakes in the past. Still, "Children, obey your parents in the Lord: for this is right. Honour thy father and mother; which is the first commandment with promise; That it may be well with thee, and thou mayest live long on the earth" (Ephesians 6:1-3). Furthermore, consider the following passage as it relates to the boss/employee relationship: "Servants, be obedient to them that are your masters according to the flesh, with fear and trembling, in singleness of your heart, as unto Christ; Not with eyeservice, as menpleasers; but as the servants of Christ, doing the will of God from the heart; With good will doing service, as to the Lord, and not to men: Knowing that whatsoever good thing any man doeth, the same shall he receive of the Lord, whether he be bond or free" (Ephesians 6:5-8 KJV).

Also, make note of this message as it relates to the government/citizen relationship:

> Let every soul be subject unto the higher powers. For there is no power but of God: the powers that be are ordained of God. Whosoever therefore resisteth the power, resisteth the ordinance of God: and they that resist shall receive to themselves damnation. For rulers are not a terror to good works, but to the evil. Wilt thou then not be afraid of the power? do that which is good, and thou shalt have praise of the same: For he is the minister of God to thee for good. But if thou do that which is evil, be afraid; for he beareth not the sword in vain: for he is the minister of God, a revenger to execute wrath upon him that doeth evil. Wherefore ye must needs be subject, not only for wrath, but also for conscience sake. For for this cause pay ye tribute also: for they are God's ministers, attending continually upon this very thing. Render therefore to all their dues: tribute to whom tribute is due; custom to whom custom; fear to whom fear; honour to whom honour (Romans 13:1-7).

Nevertheless, it is very tempting to complain, mock, and contend with an authority figure. The media, the entertainment industry (e.g., music lyrics, TV shows, etc.), and the world in general have no regard for this biblical principle. In the Old Testament, the earth could literally open and swallow alive those who dared to rebel or revile against an established authority figure (e.g., Korah's rebellion in Numbers 16:31) or even not get to live long if one disrespected a father or mother (Exodus 20:12).

Do not let yourself be fooled or influenced by the world's attitude toward those in positions of authority. The God of the Old Testament is the same God today. As to the people of Israel, ignoring this command can cause you forty years of wandering in a desert—that is, from job to job, from church to church, and in some cases, in and out of jail. *Those who do not submit themselves well to authority may not qualify for God's given gifts.*

Reflection Question

Think of a time you disrespected, reviled, or contended with someone in a position of authority and briefly describe the outcomes of such behavior.

_____

_____

_____

_____

_____

_____

_____

_____

_____

_____

_____

_____

_____

_____

_____

Quick Submission to Authority Check

Identify an authority figure for each of these areas, then place a checkmark next to the ones where your attitude toward them aligns with the Scriptures. To be subject to authority is not up to an emotion or a feeling; it is a decision that you have made as an individual. The rest is the working of the Holy Spirit.

Area of Life	Authority Figure	Compliance check
Home	_____	☐
Work	_____	☐
Government	_____	☐
School	_____	☐
Church	_____	☐

Recommended Prayer

For each unchecked authority figure in the exercise above, pray as follows:

Dear Lord Jesus, today I make the decision before You to be subject to _____ (write the names of the specific authority figure you are struggling with, such as your parent, guardian, church leader, teacher, boss, government authority, etc.). I understand that this is not only Your will, but also a requirement to fulfill my mission in life. Lord, I also repent for _____ (write the applicable tendency toward the above-mentioned authority figure, such as reviling, complaining, rebelling, contending, or scolding) against such individual, and I ask that You take control over _____ (write the particular area you are struggling with, such as a rebellious attitude, a scolding/contending tongue, etc.), for Your Word says that it is You who works in me to will and to act according to Your good purpose. And if other people are doing this before me at home, church, school, or work, I ask you to give me the courage and conviction to walk away and not take part in it, for I know now that this is not pleasing to You. Thank you, Lord. In Jesus' name. Amen.

Definitions

Contending: To strive in controversy or debate; to dispute.
Rebelling: To resist or defy an authority or a generally accepted convention.
Complaining: To express feelings of dissatisfaction or resentment.
Reviling: To assail with abusive language; vituperate.
Scolding: To reprimand or criticize harshly and usually angrily; to reprove or criticize someone or something openly.
(References: www.thefreedictionary.com)

Activity# 1

If applicable and feasible, arrange to have the following conversation with the above-mentioned individuals. The example below is just a suggestion. In most cases, discretion, judgment, and further guidance are highly recommended. This command does not condone dictatorial or abusive leadership—that is, when you are directed to act contrary to the moral principles and ethical norms prescribed in the Bible and society in general. Always remember these three things: if the situation is illegal, unethical, or immoral, don't do it. Now consider the following conversation.

(Address affected authority figure by name, avoid general remarks) _____
I want to talk to you in reference to my past behavior when I _____
(questioned, disrespected, contended, complained, or disobeyed you, be specific)
on this date_____, during_____ (a work meeting,
class, conversation, family reunion, etc.). I need you to know that my faith in
Jesus Christ compels me to acknowledge you, honor you, and respect you as my
_____ (father, mother, teacher, pastor, boss, etc.), regardless
of how I feel or think about your decisions. I need to ask you for your forgiveness,
just I asked God to forgive me for my actions that day.

Activity #2

To submit to all in positions of authority is a direct commandment of the Lord. Therefore, in this activity, you are required to write the name of your church leader. Depending on your local church organizational structure this could be your pastor, assistant pastor, deacon, or elder.

In summary, you can say that submitting to those in position of authority is to simply learn to obey your leaders by following their direction and guidance. To understand the reason for this prerequisite, you must consider the following:

> And I, behold, I have given with him Aholiab, the son of Ahisamach, of the tribe of Dan: and in the hearts of all that are wise hearted I have put wisdom, that they may make all that I have commanded thee. The tabernacle of the congregation, and the ark of the testimony, and the mercy seat that is thereupon, and all the furniture of the tabernacle. And the table and his furniture, and the pure candlestick with all his furniture, and the altar of incense. And the altar of burnt offering with all his furniture, and the laver and his foot. And the cloths of service, and the holy garments for Aaron the priest, and the garments of his sons, to minister in the priest's office. And the anointing oil, and sweet incense for the holy place: according to all that I have commanded thee shall they do (Exodus 31:6-11).

Moses passed on to Bezalel and Oholiab specific directions on how the tabernacle and its furnishings were to be built. There were very precise instructions that ranged from materials to be used, to specific measurements and designs. (See book of Exodus.) In modern terms, these directions were nothing but safety guidelines to prevent a fatal death. In the case of the tabernacle, if there was anything that was not in compliance with the given building code, the glory of God could take the life of the priest and whoever was at the altar.

Because of the severity of the consequences for not following directions, the Bible instruction is very clear: "And Samuel said, Hath the LORD as great delight in burnt offerings and sacrifices, as in obeying the voice of the LORD? Behold, to obey is better than sacrifice, and to hearken (to listen or pay attention) than the fat of rams. For rebellion is as the sin of witchcraft, and stubbornness is as iniquity and idolatry. Because thou hast rejected the word of the LORD, he hath also rejected thee from being king" (1 Samuel 15:22-23).

Here it is—the scenario. Israel was at war. Samuel was God's prophet and priest (authority figure). Saul was the king of Israel, responsible for following Samuel's instructions. In this passage, he was directed to wait for Samuel to conduct the sacrifice. This sacrifice was the determining factor as to whether Israel would win or lose the battle against the Philistines. Samuel was taking longer than he was expected, so Saul went ahead and on his own accord, decided to conduct the sacrifice himself. This was something that only priests were authorized to do. When Samuel arrived and saw what was done, he reacted in the following manner:

> And Samuel said to Saul, Thou hast done foolishly: thou hast not kept the commandment of the LORD thy God, which he commanded thee: for now would the LORD have established thy kingdom upon Israel for ever. But now thy kingdom shall not continue: the LORD hath sought him a man after his own heart, and the LORD hath commanded him to be captain over his people, because thou hast not kept that which the LORD commanded thee (1 Samuel 13:13-14).

In the Old Testament, the word of a prophet was recognized as the word of God; Saul's disobedience to Samuel's instructions was considered a fundamental violation of his career responsibilities. This incident in the life of Saul teaches us a valuable lesson. Those who tend to set their own will above the instructions received from those in a position of authority cease to be an instrument of the Lord and carry the risk of being set aside from his purpose, for the teaching of pastors, teachers, and mentors God would send into their lives to equip them for the work ahead would not have any effect in them whatsoever.

Listen to advice and accept instruction, that you may gain wisdom in the future. (Proverbs 19:20 ESV). The requirements of submitting to authority and obeying instructions teaches us that even though you could have the best intentions in the world, but fail regularly and carelessly to follow instructions, there is a risk of being replaced by someone else. There is nothing personal against such individuals; it is simply the fact that those in leadership positions have the responsibility to ensure that their organizations run effectively towards their goals, for in many cases, depending on the situation, the stakes are high and costly, and can affect other people as well. Because of this, anyone who expects to receive a God-given gift is required to pay attention (take heed) and to follow (obey) the guidance received from their parents, pastors, teachers, employer, and mentors as to the specific decisions/actions they need to make. Always remember that your work is a critical link within the team effort to reach sinners. (These are the same motives of the tabernacle, and the same motives behind Israel's victory against its enemies in the passage just read).

Activity #3

The Bible states that to obey is better than any sacrifice you can give to God, and that to pay attention is better than the fat of rams. Describe a situation where you failed to follow directions given by an authority figure. As you recall the incident, try to identify the factors that prompted you to not follow the directions that were given, as well as some of the things you could have done differently to prevent it. Examples may include the following: a lack of organization (not using an agenda or daily planner), lack of prioritizing skills, lack of training or knowledge of the task, or an arrogant attitude that does not ask questions for clarification.

Remember, "God resisteth the proud, but giveth grace unto the humble" (James 4:6). To be humble is to recognize and accept that there is an issue that needs to be fixed and to ask for help. Following directions is a mandatory skill for all who want to receive their career gift, so fix whatever it is that you need to fix and implement whatever system you need to implement to follow directions accurately. There are no excuses; your career depends on it.

This is what the Bible says about procrastinating (to put off something that needs to be taken care of, especially out of carelessness and laziness): "He also that is slothful in his work is brother to him that is a great waster" (Proverbs 18:9). What you are destroying in this case is the opportunity to be used by God in the proclamation of the Gospel. It's a serious matter of life and death, like in the case of building the tabernacle per God's instructions.

_____

_____

_____

_____

_____

_____

_____

_____

_____

_____

Activity #4: Becoming Good at Following Directions

For this activity, you are required to write the instructions you have received from your church leader on how you are to support your local church mission. If you are not active in your local church (Prerequisite 1), then this is the time to get involved and start receiving some instructions to follow. Only through practice is how you become good at following directions.

_____

_____

_____

_____

_____

_____

_____

_____

_____

_____

_____

_____

_____

_____

Notes

3

Learn to Receive Discipline and Correction with Humility

After Saul's removal, God appointed David as king. He testified concerning him: "I have found David the son of Jesse, a man after mine own heart, which shall fulfil all my will" (Acts 13:22). Why did God refer to David as a man after his own heart when he, indeed, also made huge mistakes? (See the life of David in the books of Samuel.) Because what set David apart from Saul was his attitude. David accepted responsibility for his mistakes, not only repenting for his actions, but also receiving discipline and correction with humility.

To repent means to feel regret over one's action and to change one's mind. Saul never truly repented, nor received correction; instead, he provided excuses consisting of self-justification and shifting of blame to others. To God, this attitude represented that Saul was going to keep failing to follow instructions and disrespecting authority and this kind of attitude, in a war, was a matter of life and death to the Israeli army. Therefore, the Bible incorporates David's attitude as the last prerequisite for a God-given career gift: Learn to receive discipline and correction with humility.

The Scriptures state that: "He that refuseth instruction despiseth his own soul: but he that heareth reproof getteth understanding…and before honour is humility" (Proverbs 15:32-33). "If ye be willing and obedient, ye shall eat the good of the land [as for career opportunities], but if ye refuse and rebel, ye shall be devoured with the sword" (Isaiah 1:20). Notice that this is exactly how Saul ended his life. He killed himself with his own sword. (See 1 Samuel 31:4). This goes to show you how far the consequences of not receiving correction and discipline with humility can go.

This refers to an individual who hates discipline and correction of any kind, who is quick to quarrel and give full vent to his or her anger. In the present time, failure to comply with this principle will cause you to be devoured by a different kind of sword, although still your own sword; namely, the self- destructive sword of stubbornness, egocentrism, and arrogance (a form of idolatry) (See 1 Samuel 15:22-23). Think of it as if you were an Olympic athlete. Would an athlete who does not follow instructions or receive the discipline and correction from his or her coach have any chance of winning the Olympics? Most likely not.

This principle will have the same effect in your career if you reject the correction and discipline received from those in position of authority, such as your teachers, parents, pastors, and mentors. The principle of receiving correction with humility refers to those who are complacent and trust more in their own opinions than on the commandment of the Lord: "Do you see a man wise in his own eyes? There is more hope for a fool than for him" (Proverbs 26:12 NKJV). Contrary to this self-destructive behavior, a man or woman after God's own heart is a disciple who embraces an attitude of obedience (follows direction) and humility (accepts correction). This is the kind of attitude that will position your gift in God's intended career path, as you apply and follow with diligence the instructions and guidance received from God's leaders, mentors, and teachers—the attitude that sets the environment for learning, professional growth, and for God to use you in the fulfillment of His mission.

To receive correction and discipline with humility means to take responsibility for one's own actions (no excuses). Accept correction and discipline without getting upset or feeling offended, and you must learn from the mistakes made by diligently and responsibly taking steps to prevent future occurrences. Saul provided excuses: "When I saw that men were scattering, and that you did not come at the set time…. I felt compelled to offer the burnt offering" (1 Samuel 13:11-12). And then he ran to see a psychic to tell him his future: "For rebellion is like the sin of divination" (1 Samuel 15:22-23). David, on the other hand, said to God: "For I know my transgressions, and my sin is always before me. Against you, you only, have I sinned and done what is evil in your sight" (Psalm 51:3). Is your heart like David's heart? If not, ask God to mold your heart like David's, and the Holy Spirit will do the work if you allow Him.

Practice Exercise

In the space below, write some corrections you have received in the last six months from someone in a position of authority. Then, for each instance, identify what measures you can take to correct the issues that were addressed, and include the instructions that were given for improvement.

_____

_____

_____

_____

_____

_____

_____

_____

Notes

Notes

Investor Approach to Career Discovery and Planning
(Adopting an investor approach to God's given gift)

Consider the following parable.

> For it will be like a man going on a journey, who called his servants and entrusted to them his property. To one he gave five talents, to another two, to another one, to each according to his ability. Then he went away. He who had received the five talents went at once and traded with them, and he made five talents more. So also, he who had the two talents made two talents more. But he who had received the one talent went and dug in the ground and hid his master's money. Now after a long time the master of those servants came and settled accounts with them. And he who had received the five talents came forward, bringing five talents more, saying, "Master, you delivered to me five talents; here I have made five talents more." His master said to him, "Well done, good and faithful servant. You have been faithful over a little; I will set you over much. Enter into the joy of your master." And he also who had the two talents came forward, saying, "Master, you delivered to me two talents; here I have made two talents more." His master said to him, "Well done, good and faithful servant. You have been faithful over a little; I will set you over much. Enter into the joy of your master." He also who had received the one talent came forward, saying, "Master, I knew you to be a hard man, reaping where you did not sow, and gathering where you scattered no seed, so I was afraid, and I went and hid your talent in the ground. Here you have what is yours." But his master answered him, "You wicked and slothful servant! You knew that I reap where I have not sown and gather where I scattered no seed? Then you ought to have invested my money with the bankers, and at my coming I should have received what was my own with interest" (Matthew 25:14-27 ESV).

A steward here is a person put in charge of a large estate, an administrator of finances and property. The term is a job title for someone with certain duties toward the property owner. In the context of career planning, God is the property/gift owner; you are a manager or steward of His gift. Why did the Bible use this term? Simply because God expects you to apply the same principles of investing to the career gift He is going to deposit in you, just as stewards used to do in biblical times to protect, manage, and increase their lord's business operation.

The main point of the parable of the talents is that God demands the kind of stewardship that produces results within God's mission. The term *talent* was first used as a unit of weight (about seventy-five pounds). Then later it was used as a unit of coinage. In the present time, the term is used to indicate a natural ability. Whether the term is interpreted as money or as a natural ability, a talent represents a given "power." The word *power* means an ability to do or act on behalf of something. Therefore, a talent is a God-given power to impact God's mission. A closer look at this parable reveals the following three points:

1. God entrusted you with a gift that belonged to Him: "Called his servants and entrusted his property to them" (Matthew 25:14 NKJV).

2. The gifts are distributed based on the individual's ability: "To one he gave five talents of money, to another two talents, and to another one talent, each according to his ability" (Matthew 25:15). An individual's ability is not determined by the person's IQ or physical make up, but by the intent of his or her heart and by his or her label of faith or commitment to God's mission. "For where your treasure is, there your heart will be also" (Luke 12:34). "The Lord does not look at things man looks at. Man looks at the outward appearance, but the Lord looks at the heart" (1 Samuel 16:7).

3. God looks at the motivation of the heart and commitment to His mission in the same way that a farmer looks for good soil for his crop as a prediction of a successful harvest. In other words, God looks at a person's potential based on the individual's faith, obedience, commitment to the Church, and most importantly, his or her personal relationship with Him. The filling of the Spirit of God comes first, then comes the ability and knowledge. "I have filled him with the Spirit of God, with skill, ability, and knowledge in all kinds of crafts" (Exodus 31:3).

Per the parable of the talents, you are going to be accountable for what you accomplish with the level of power you have received (two, three, five talents). The more power you have received, the greater the impact to God's mission and the higher level of the accountability you will have. To be accountable means to be liable and able to explain one's actions. God applies an investor approach to his gifts, which explains why the hidden talent was given to the one with ten talents: "Take the talent from him and give it to the one who has the ten talents" (Matthew 25:28). This is the most effective approach to guarantee a higher return on investment. "For everyone that has will be given more, and he will have abundance. Whoever does not have, even what he has will be taken away even that which he hath" (Matthew 25:29 KJV). To hide a talent on the ground (see Matthew 25:25) is to use God's entrusted property (your unique career gift) for one's own personal success and advancement instead of using it for God's mission.

This passage teaches us that we have a duty toward the Giver of all talents. The career planning steps you are about to learn flow out of this responsibility to ensure that you deliver the results that the Master and King of all expects for His investments. This being said, your God-given career gift is going to be manifested when you approach the career planning process with an investor attitude following the prerequisites you've learned thus far. In this last section, you will learn the five simple steps that will lead you to the discovery of the career ability God has already deposited in you, if you have done the following:

✓ Become an active member of the Church
✓ Learned to submit to authority
✓ Learned to receive discipline and correction with humility

Before we get started, we must consider that the Bible teaches us to establish a support network with the following instruction: "By wisdom a house is built and through understanding it is established; through knowledge its rooms are filled with rare and beautiful treasures. A wise man has great power, and a man of knowledge increases strength; for waging war you need guidance, and for victory many advisers" (Proverbs 24: 3-6 NKJV). Also, you must remember that "through knowledge its rooms are filled with rare and beautiful treasures." (Proverbs 24:4). *Treasures* are the valuable information, guidance, wisdom, and life-changing advice one receives from other people, including lessons learned from one's own mistakes and on-the-job experiences. "For wisdom is better than rubies; and all the things that may be desired are not compared to it" (Proverbs 8:11). *Rooms* refers to the different steps of the investor approach to career planning you are about to learn.

Moreover, humility is the foundation for career knowledge and wisdom: "When pride cometh, then cometh shame: but with the lowly is wisdom" (Proverbs 11:2). Humility takes place when the individual first accepts the fact that he or she doesn't know it all and can't do everything by him or herself, seeking guidance/assistance for every decision. Secondly, the individual can be obedient to the teaching received from others (mentors) and to the lessons learned through experience: "The way of a fool is right in his own eyes, but a wise man is he who listens to counsel" (Proverbs 12:15 NASB).

This was the real purpose of the prerequisites you just learned. Therefore, each step identifies a **subject matter expert (Helpers).** These are the professionals with the training and experience to guide you through every step of the process, creating a collaboration platform where multiple areas of expertise synchronize themselves to achieve a defined objective; that is, each step goal. When step five is reached, you are going to be able to clearly identify God's given gifts, as promised.

What are the leading industries where I live? (Step 1)

Knowing the leading industries that are present where you live is how you find out which career gives a higher return for your gift (just like an investor).

Most employers belong to an industry sector or a national professional association that identifies them and sets the rules of their game, figuratively speaking. An industry or professional field is the classification (or separation) of businesses according to the type of service or product they provide to the people. For example, a business that sells cars is in a separate category than a business that does banking or provides health care.

Having a career does not mean that you picked an occupation in which you will be working for the rest of your life. Instead, it means that you chose an industry or professional field in which to take part. A search in the dictionary reveals the following definitions:

Career: *A profession pursued as a permanent calling; a course of continued progress or activity.*
Occupation: *Duties/tasks; a job position at which one regularly works for pay.*

You choose a career when you decide the type of *service* or *product* you want to contribute to society (permanent calling… continued progress). That is deciding what type of industry to be part of, and <u>not</u> choosing an occupation. Occupations are job positions within the industry. Let's look at some examples.

Careers	Occupations
(A chosen Industry)	(What you do within the industry, your role or function)
Health Care Industry	Nurse, nurse assistant, physician, health administrator, X-ray technician, physical therapist, etc.
Finance Industry	Teller, loan officer, relationship banker, financial advisor, insurance agent, etc.
Education Industry	Elementary teacher, school principal, college associate professor, school administrator, etc.

Step 1 sets parameters on career exploration in a way that leads you to choose industries that tap into consumer demand, just as an investor would do. Consumer demand is what people want and want to pay for, and it refers to a service or product. It is also considered the fuel that keeps your career going forward, just like gasoline in a car.

You find consumer demand by simply taking a closer look at the businesses around your area. Businesses are strategically located as a response to consumer demand and the unique characteristics of the area that make it favorable for the type of industry (e.g., natural resources, export-import infrastructure [basic physical and organizational structures and facilities, such as buildings, roads, and power supplies needed for the operation of an enterprise], and demographics [statistical data relating to the population and particular groups within it], as well as other factors specific to industries).

When you do industry research of your local economy, you are taking advantage of the fact that the experts in consumer demand and commercial developers have already done 50 percent of your career planning legwork for you. Through their behind-the-scenes findings, these business experts are showing you the industries/careers that you need to focus on. When career exploration is <u>not</u> set within the limits of industry presence, career planning is like finding a needle in a haystack, and the trick to finding that needle is to reduce the size of the haystack. There are <u>thousands</u> of possible occupations, some of them constantly appearing and disappearing, but there are a little over a hundred almost unchanging industries. This much smaller number is further reduced as you discover that not all these industries are present where you live.

Defining the Area where you Live

The investor approach to career planning leads you to establish contact with employers in your community as early as 9th grade. To do this, you must be able to show up on time for any interaction. Draw a radius of one hour maximum of commuting time from where you live; this will define your area.

But, what happens if you move after graduation? If you move after graduation, you have nothing to lose. If the same industries are present where you move to, then there is no harm done. But if there are different industries, then there are always skills that can transfer from one industry to another (e.g., customer service skills, office technology, report writing skills, oral communication, etc.). Also, early career accomplishments, such as letters, commendations, and employer recognition, follow you wherever you go. In any situation, you will be better off than having no work experience at all. However, if you live in a rural area, you should include the nearest major city in your industry research.

Step 1 Helpers - Economists

To answer Step 1's question, you are going to need the assistance of economists and local government agencies. Economists study the production and distribution of goods and services. They collect and analyze data, research trends, and evaluate economic issues. Like doctors, they take an X-ray of your area and tell you where job opportunities are (strong industry sectors with a positive outlook) and where there could be trouble (weakening industries).

To answer Step 1's question, you have to list the industries operating in your area (one-hour maximum of commuting time, to include a nearby major city). If you live close to a county or city line, you may have to access more than one local government agency. You can access economists' reports and commentaries for free by visiting your county or city's official website. Once on the website, look for headers or links with titles such as: Economic Development, Labor Market Report, Analysis of Current Economic Trends, Economic & Demographics Profiles, etc.

Also, it is important to incorporate your findings into your high school course selection as soon as possible. For example, an economic note on Miami-Dade County (South Florida) states that Miami's economy is based on tourism and export/import, being considered the bridge between the continental United States and Latin America. Based just on this piece of information, wouldn't you think that to be employable in Miami, you are going to need Spanish and Portuguese as a second language, and that perhaps this is something you can learn while in school? Even if you move out of Miami, don't you get a "choose option #2 for Spanish" every time you dial a 1-800 number? This is one of the many examples of things you can find during industry research on which you can act to make yourself employable while still in high school.

Industry Research Activity

Instructions: Visit http://www.bls.gov/iag/tgs/iag_index_alpha.htm for a complete list of industries, with their corresponding NAIC code. Then, using the local resources, eliminate from the list the industries that are <u>NOT</u> present where you live. **NAICS** stands for the North American Industry Classification System, a standard system used by the government to classify business institutions according to the services they provide. *At the end of this activity, you should be able to come up with a list of the industries that are present in the area where you live.* Look at the sample provided to see how it is supposed to look, including notes and reminders you can write for yourself.

Employment area: Miami-Dade County (South Florida)

Websites/ Resources:
http://www.miamidade.gov/business/economic-development.asp
http://www.beaconcouncil.com/
Industries Found

Air Transportation (NAICS 481)
- Repair and Maintenance
- Air operations

Trade and Logistics

Retail Trade (NAICS 44-45)
- Motor Vehicle and Parts Dealers (NAICS 441)
- Furniture and Home Furnishings Stores (NAICS 442)
- Electronics and Appliance Stores (NAICS 443)
- Building Material and Garden Equipment and Supplies Dealers (NAICS 444)
- Food and Beverage Stores (NAICS 445)
- Health and Personal Care Stores (NAICS 446)
- Gasoline Stations (NAICS 447)
- Clothing and Clothing Accessories Stores (NAICS 448)
- General Merchandise Stores (NAICS 452)
- Miscellaneous Store Retailers (NAICS 453)
- Non-store Retailers (NAICS 454)
- Merchant Wholesalers Durable goods (cars, furniture, industrial equipment, etc.) (NAICS 423)
- Merchant Wholesalers Non-durable goods (paper products, chemical products, drugs, textile products, apparel, footwear, etc.) (NAICS 424)

Logistics
- Warehousing and Storage (NAICS 493)
- Wholesale Electronic Markets and Agents and Brokers (NAICS 425)

- Wholesale Trade (NAICS 42)
- Truck Transportation (NAICS 484)

Note: Every region of the world is present in Miami's international trade and logistics network. There are about 300 freight forwarders and customs broker companies.

Health Care Services

- Ambulatory Health Services (NAICS 621)
- Health Care and Social Assistance (NAICS 452)
- Hospitals (NAICS 622)
- Nursing and Residential Care Facilities (NAICS 623)

Note: Miami is home to leaders in the health care industry, such as Beckman Coulter, BD Biosciences, Cordis (a Johnson & Johnson Company), and Merck.

Hospitality and Leisure

- Accommodation and Food Services (NAICS 72)
- Food Services and Drinking Places (NAICS 722)

Note: Miami is considered one of the top urban resorts in the world and a favored location for business meetings, sales events, and trade shows, including high-profile political and religious events.

Banking and Finance

- Finance and Insurance (NAICS 52)
- Funds, Trusts, and other financial vehicles (NAICS 525)

Note: Miami has the largest concentration of domestic and international banks on the East Coast after New York City. It includes private banking and wealth management and trade finance.

Professional Services

- Legal Services (NAICS 5411)
- Accounting, Tax Preparation, Bookkeeping, and Payroll Services (NAICS 5412)
- Architectural, Engineering, and Related Services (NAICS 5413)
- Specialized Design Services (NAICS 5414)
- Computer Systems Design and Related Services (NAICS 5415)
- Management, Scientific, and Technical Consulting Services (NAICS 5416)
- Advertising and Related Services (NAICS 5418)
- Real Estate and Rental and Leasing (NAICS 53)
- Administrative and Support Services (NAICS 561)

- Repair and Maintenance (NAICS 811)
    - o Automotive Repair and Maintenance (NAICS 8111)
    - o Electronic and Precision Equipment Repair and Maintenance (NAICS 8112)
    - o Commercial and Industrial Machinery and Equipment (except Automotive and Electronic) Repair and Maintenance (NAICS 8113)

With a simple online research, you and your parents are going to be able to considerably reduce the size of the possible career haystack. In the sample provided, this Miami student was able to bring down his career options to about 43 possible industries, including subsectors. This number of possible careers can be further reduced; in Step 2, coming up next, you will learn how this is done.

Which of these leading industries am I interested in? (Step 2)

The key word in this question is *interested*. Interest is defined as:

1. The state of wanting to know about something.
2. The quality of making someone curious or holding their attention.

Consider this following illustration. Imagine for a second that you had to pick a class that would never end and that you would never graduate from. Wouldn't you want to make sure to pick a subject that would make you curious and want to know more? These classes do exist; grownups call it continuing education. Continuing education means you will be bound to study the same subject until your mid-seventies (possible retirement age, according to the social security office projections).

Picture this for a second; at eight o'clock in the morning, as soon as you report to work, you will read hundreds of emails about this same subject, then, the phone will ring and people will start asking you questions and talking about their problems with, you guessed it… the same subject. Choosing an industry based on interest is how you ensure that you are going to stay motivated and focused in school and at work. Interest influences your academic and work performance, and both employers and post-secondary schools will consider your performance and accomplishments when choosing one candidate over another. The essential point is that interest should be your motivation to enter a particular industry; however, you won't know if something is interesting until you test it out.

Talking about testing things out, in the following illustration you can see how testing a career is a very similar process to buying a new car. The first step of car buying is to determine your budget (how much you can afford). Once you figure out that number, you are going to make a list of cars available within the boundaries of your budget. In Step 1, you did something similar, when you came up with a list of possible careers within the limits or boundaries of consumer demand, namely, industry presence.

Second, the car buyer researches online each of these models, to see which of them catches their **interest** (e.g., looks at photos and reads tons of information about the car). Did you know that 80 percent of car buyers research different cars online for several months before they decide to walk into a car dealership? In this same way, you are going to research each of these industries online before you go to the actual field to contact an employee in the industry or embark on what this book calls a "career test drive."

As you go through the Industry of Interest Activity coming up next, use interest to progressively eliminate industries from the list you created in Step 1. Interest can be uncovered by asking questions like the ones found below:

- What kind of problems do you like to solve? For example, neighbors are always coming to you so you can fix their computer.
- What kind of questions do people come to you for help with? For what services or products? For example, friends call you all the time to ask you what software program they should buy for their computer.

- What is the most typical topic that would get started in a conversation? For example, the latest informational technology news.
- When you are in the magazine section of a library/bookstore, what type of magazine do you usually pick up? For example: *PC World*, *TechNews*, or any other technology publication.
- As you go through the "finding your interest" activities, ask yourself what experience you enjoyed the most. What made it so? For example, going to a technology trade show and watching demonstrations of the latest technology.
- What academic subjects do you prefer in school? For example: computer science.

Industry of Interest Activity

Imagine if you were test driving careers at the occupational level; how long would that take? Some online occupational databases boast of having about 20,000-plus occupations. Before you and you parents get on the road, wasting time and gasoline, there are some industries that can be eliminated from the comfort of your home or nearby library. Here are some recommendations:

1. Research online for information about each of the industries listed in Step 1. Look at the product and/or service they provide to the people. You can start by simply typing the name of the industry in the search box of any search engine (e.g., Google, Yahoo, YouTube, etc.). There is no fixed amount of time to spend on each industry. Some of them you will know right away, and some others might take you a little longer. Always give yourself plenty time with each industry and consult various sources. As you are doing this research, ask yourself, do I want to read more about this? If the answer is no, cross out that industry from your list. But if the answer is yes, proceed to item 2.

2. In your local library, look for industry magazines and journals. In these publications, you can not only read about hot topics and pressing issues in the industry, but also find articles about leading professionals in the field and company profiles (go back at least one year of publication). Also read ads, marketing brochures, news bulletins, and subscribe to the publication's newsletter and its Internet blog (participate in their forums and ask questions). Still wanting to learn more? Eliminate some from your industry list and from those that remain, take it a step further.

3. Search for the professional associations these industries belong to. Use the Encyclopedia of Associations available online or in any public library. For example, students interested in accounting (as in the professional service industry) can visit the American Institute of Certified Public Accountants at www.aicpa.org. Once on the association page, look to see what informational material, programs, or training they have for students interested in the industry. Usually this information is found on the career tab of the site's home page. Also check out what conferences, conventions, trade shows, and seminars you can attend. Meet current employees at all levels, from CEO down, and visit booths to collect informational material. Networking starts here (see section on Networking). After all this is done, ask yourself again: which of these industries am I still interested in? As you answer this question, some industries will be crossed out, but some will remain.

4. By now you should have a manageable number of possible industries of interest (3 to 5, if not fewer). Now it makes sense to drive around town for an informational interview (see section below). After the informational interviews, decide which of them you would like to take for a career test drive.

5. For those industries that passed the informational interview (a much smaller number of industries by this time), conduct a career test drive, commonly referred to as job shadowing (read section below) and/or volunteer work (if the industry allows for it, such as in the case of the health care industry).

6. Lastly, get an industry of interest confirmation check-out from a certified career coach.

Step 2 Helpers - Career Coaches

The Finding your Industry of Interest activity can generate an overwhelming amount of indecision, especially when it comes to whether to leave in or eliminate an industry. Therefore, you need to reach out to a career coach. They are the ones with the training and experience to help you succeed in this step. Most students think that career coaching is about helping people find a job when they can't find one on their own. However, their interest inventories assessments, which includes feedback from people who know you well, is the most effective tool available that can help you sort out and interpret all those interesting indicators you've collected thus far. Just like when you go to the doctor, you must be able to talk about your symptoms and what you feel; there has to be a previous career exposure to give your career coach something to work with.

This book makes a distinction between a "cold" interest inventory assessment and a "hot" one. Wouldn't it be easier for a person to decide on a car if he or she had the opportunity to test drive it first? Likewise, in a hot interest inventory assessment, you already possess an industry experience to rely on as you move to the interest assessment questions, while in a cold one there are no previous references other than your own mentally constructed sense of reality (a reality that, because of lack of exposure, can be very far from the truth). In a hot interest inventory assessment, the interest indicators you experienced are verified and confirmed, providing the career coach the information about you that he or she needs to help point you to your industry of interest. Once your industry of interest has been determined, you are going to document it in your Career Worksheet.

Networking

Networking is the act of <u>interacting</u> with individuals who have a certain expertise, to build relationships that will produce current and future benefits. The benefit of this means you'll glean industry information. For that industry information to get to you, there must be a communication channel already in placed between you and current employees of the industry of interest. The investor approach to career planning requires students to make a career decision on accurate industry information; therefore, learning about networking is highly encouraged. Constantly ask in your social and family circle if they know somebody you may contact who works in any of the industries you are considering. Update your Network Contact Sheet as you meet people. Here are some questions you can ask your family and friends:

Do you know someone who knows the person I want to see for _____?
(Example: name of the industry)

Do you know anyone who works for _____? (Example: name of an employer)

Can you give me the name of the hiring decision maker for _____?
(Example: specific local office of an employer you're thinking of working for)

Informational Interview

You may want to hold off on informational interviews for Item 5 of Finding your Industry of Interest Activity until after you have learned everything you can from other resources. The objective is to get the answers you could not get anywhere else. Here are some recommendations and sample questions:

1. Be selective with whom you speak. Try to talk to people well-known in the industry who have been successful, preferably the ones who are considered experts in the field, with 10-plus years of experience.
2. Do research on the person you are going to interview. See what you can learn about his or her education and experience. This will give you a better idea of what to ask, and the person will be impressed by the fact that you took time to research them. Search for their professional profile on LinkedIn or on their employer's website.
3. Try to schedule the interview at the individual's actual worksite for an accurate picture of the industry environment.
4. Arrive on time (or up to ten minutes early) for your meeting or make the phone call as scheduled.
5. Do not schedule the meeting for more than 20 minutes.
6. Do not exceed your scheduled meeting time unless the person indicates it is okay to do so.
7. Organize your thoughts before the meeting and plan your follow-up question as appropriate.
8. Ask the most important questions first in case you run out of time.
9. Send a formal thank you note following the interview.

Informational interviews question samples:

- What do you see happening in the industry in the next five years?
- What changes are occurring in the industry right now?
- What challenges are facing the industry?
- If you were in my position, how would you go about getting into the industry?
- What next steps do you recommend if I was interested in the industry?
- Is there any specific internship or volunteer work opportunity that you recommend for those interested in the industry? (Talk about the possibility of job shadowing.)
- <u>May I contact you if other questions arise?</u>
- <u>Can you refer me to other people in the industry I could also talk to?</u>

Again, ask questions for which answers are not available on other sources. For example, you don't want to ask for general information that is posted on the company's website. However, you can take this opportunity to verify information you found online or to request clarification on a certain issue about the industry that you don't fully understand. The underlined questions are mandatory, as they establish a network channel for more interviewing as required in the steps to follow.

Job Shadowing

Job shadowing is short-term, unpaid exposure to the actual workplace of an occupation. Here, the student gets to follow an employee through his or her workday. However, the objective of this activity is for the student to learn about the industry they are considering in general terms, not focus on a specific occupation (Step 5 will deal with specific occupation job shadowing). The focus of job shadowing in Step 2 is for you to gain exposure to the different interactions and processes involved in the daily operation of a business (the overall working environment).

Get information from your high school counselor about job shadowing programs available. If there are any, request the school administration to coordinate this activity. Make sure to get your parents involved if you want something to get done.

Job Shadowing Worksheet

You may use the worksheet below to organize your findings and give you an idea of what kind of information you need to collect.

Information to be collected	**Findings**

What are the employer's mission and core values?

What are the employer's top priorities?

Note: This may include new projects, goals, and/or initiatives.

What job positions are involved in the daily business operation? What are their roles within the operation and how do they support each other?

Look for the following:

Who depends on or benefits from each job position?

Are there any support roles? (Positions that help keep the organization running smoothly but aren't directly associated with either making or selling a product/service, such as administrative assistant, receptionist, etc.)

Who are the vendors or suppliers that the industry depends on?

Note: A vendor is a company that provides a service or a product that is needed in the operation of the business (e.g., office supplies, raw materials, parts suppliers, etc.)

What equipment, tools, materials, and/or technology are used?

What are the physical characteristics of the worksite?
Examples:
Location (e.g., indoors, or outdoors)
Work space (e.g., office, shop, laboratory)
Atmosphere (e.g., calm versus bustling)
Physical conditions (e.g., clean versus dirty)

What are the major challenges and problems that the employer is currently facing in the industry?
Example: issues affecting the employer's productivity and ability to compete in the industry, etc.

Step 2 Helpers - High School Counselor

Once you have determined your industry of interest, you are going to let your high school counselor know. He or she is going to assist you with the selection of classes according to the applicable career cluster. The U.S. Department of Education's 16 Career Clusters provide schools with a way of structuring their curriculum so that students can take classes around a particular professional field or industry. When you select a career cluster from the list below, you learn about that field along with your general academics (i.e., English, mathematics, social studies, and science) and within the context of that career field.

Since there are several occupations associated with each cluster, the skills learned are usually transferable from one related occupation to another, if they belong to the same career cluster (e.g., business, management, and administration). Once you select a career cluster, your high school guidance counselor can help you select the elective courses that will progress you further in your knowledge of the chosen field. Your ability to make wise course selections within an industry in high school will contribute to your success later in a chosen secondary school (college/vocational school) or even the workforce, since you are going to be building on the foundation of previous knowledge for that particular industry.

1. Agriculture, food and natural resources
2. Architecture and construction
3. Arts, audio/video technology and communications
4. Business, management, and administration
5. Education and training
6. Finance
7. Government and public administration
8. Health science
9. Hospitality and tourism
10. Human services
11. Information technology
12. Law, public safety, and security
13. Manufacturing
14. Marketing, sales, and services
15. Science, technology, engineering, and mathematics
16. Transportation, distribution, and logistics

Who are the leading employers in the industry I have chosen? (Step 3)

In this step, you are going to identify the top employers of your industry of interest. Therefore, in the search box of any of the search engines or business directories listed in the activity below, type the service or product that your industry of interest is known for (e.g., accounting, legal services, banks, doctor's office, etc.); then, select your city/area and click the search button. You may also use the industry name as per the NAICS classification, or phrases that include the name of the service and the area combined (e.g., accounting firms in Miami-Dade County, or auto shops in zip code 33165). Once the Employer List Activity is completed, you may proceed to Step 4.

Employer Name	Contact Information (website, phone, address)	Contact Person (job title, phone, e-mail)	Employer Description (who they are and what they do)
Brown & Brown Accounting Services	www.brownandbrowntax.com Phone: 555-555-5555 Address: 12345 SW 158 Ave. Miami, Florida 33125	John White – Human Resources manager Phone: 305 555-5555 Ext 123 E-mail: john@brownandbrown.com	Large tax preparation company with offices in all 50 states and overseas. Offers banking, payroll, personal finance, and business consulting services.
Smith & Company, P.A.	(No website) Phone: 888-888-8888 Address: 6789 SW 222 Ave. Miami, Florida 33125	Joe Black – Office manager. Phone: 888-888-8888 Ext. 345 E-mail: Joe@smithandcompany.com	Small accounting firm serving the West Miami area. Offers income tax preparation for businesses and individuals, as well as bookkeeping and payroll services.

Note: These two examples are based on Accounting, Tax Preparation, Bookkeeping, and Payroll Services (NAICS 5412) as the Industry of Interest.

Employer List Activity

Instructions: Keep the number of employers to a manageable number. For example, if there are more than 100 accounting firms in your area, contact 10 to 20 of them. Start with the ones closer to you, working out until you reach the one-hour-of-commuting radius. Use online business directories and search engines such as: http://www.google.com; http://local.yahoo.com; http://www.bing.com/businessportal; http://www.yellowpages.com; http://www.yelp.com; and http://manta.com. Also, keep in mind three basic criteria as a set of guidelines for discovering the leading employer for each industry:

- Criteria for large corporations
- Criteria for small businesses
- Criteria for non-profit institutions and government entities

Criteria for Leading Large Corporations: The Employee-Investor Approach

The criteria for leading large corporations involves a search for companies in the best position, as of available resources, to develop your skills and talents. This process involves an analysis of the company's financial condition, like the one conducted by an investor considering buying stocks of a company. Competitive sales revenue increases are a direct result of effective management, an empowered workforce, and innovative research efforts that keep informed of consumer demand. These factors create opportunities for the kind of training and exposure to proven business practices that will make your skills flourish. Simply put, these market leaders will provide you the performance-based model you need to shape your career.

Criteria for Small Professional Businesses: The "Hiring a Mentor" Approach

These criteria apply to small businesses such as law firms, family medicine practices, insurance agents, and contractors (e.g., plumbing services, electricians, etc.). The objective here is to teach you to look for mentors who could introduce you and guide you through the industry learning process. Symbolically speaking, this process is indicative of hiring a mentor. In the category of small businesses, market leadership is determined by establishing criteria for the industry. This process includes a closer look at the owner's professional profile, which incorporates the individual's years of professional experience, certifications obtained, distinguishable career accomplishments, projects involved, and local reputation.

The industry research question to answer for small businesses is: Which of these local professionals would contribute the most to my career, based on their professional profile? A mentor is a wise and trusted counselor or teacher, an influential senior sponsor/supporter; someone willing to pass along his or her industry knowledge and skills to someone eager to learn and appreciate the value of it—you, in this case. Mentors are facilitators of professional growth; the main reason you are seeking employment with them.

Generally, someone who has already achieved a significant level of professional success within the business is the best candidate to show you how to get there. The benefits of being part of a successful professional's work team may include the following:

- Opportunity for networking within the industry, as you benefit from your mentor's already established reputation and are referred by him or her to others in the business
- Awareness of professional issues and challenges, as well as exposure to different approaches to dealing with them effectively
- Performance feedback and recommendations for improvement based on proven business practices, as well as opportunities for career coaching

The "hiring a mentor" strategy also has a component of long-term investing in the sense that when you are looking for this type of leadership, you are considering future partnership or an investing opportunity upon your mentor's retirement, capitalizing on the business's already established professional reputation.

Criteria for Non-profit Organization/Government Institutions

When it comes to considering non-profit organizations and government agencies for a career, industry research should focus on determining the following:

- Size of population receiving or desiring the service
- Source of funding
- Level of priority (how important, relevant, or critical the service is)

The size factor for the recipients of the service stipulates that the larger the population the institution serves, the more opportunities you have for developing your skills. This is also true when you are considering the source of funding. Generally, the larger the pool of taxpayers or contributors, the greater the potential for career growth.

For instance, someone working for a local government agency has fewer opportunities than someone who works for the federal government. In this case, the service rendered is expanded throughout the nation. It is not limited to county boundaries, and the source of funding is much larger.

Lastly, the level of priority relates to the allocation of limited resources within the different levels of government and non-profit organizations. The question to ask yourself at this stage is: How critical or relevant is the institution's service to the community? Financial resources will always be allocated based on priority, which means that if you land a career in an organization whose services are not critical or a priority to the community, you will receive insufficient funding, and this represents fewer career opportunities in general. For instance, a family health program may take precedence on a given local budget over a project concerned with cultural development. As you can see, everything goes back to demand, and demand is linked to funding. If there is no potential for funding, there is very limited career development. In this category, you are to direct your industry research efforts so that you can find organizations with the right budget to invest in your skills.

Additional Resources

Because the business-investor theory incorporates investing principles into the career planning process, consider the counseling of a financial advisor/analyst as part of your decision support team. A certain level of expertise is required for conducting a company's fundamental analysis, which helps you in setting market leaders apart. Such analysis serves the purpose of determining which market leader is in better financial shape, as in resources to invest in your skills.

For instance, favorable sales reports could be an indication that the company is tapping into market demand efficiently, which translates to effective management, training for its employees, product innovation, and performance-based business practices that will benefit your career development. If the collaboration with a financial advisor is not feasible, reading books and articles on the subject is highly recommended.

- The Forbes Global 2000 is an annual ranking of the top two thousand publicly traded companies around world and is sponsored by Forbes. The ranking is based on a combination of four metrics: sales numbers, profit, assets, and market value. Global 2000 and its domestic version, Forbes 500, can be used as an indicator of market leadership. Both sources are accessible by visiting www.forbes.com/global2000 and www.forbes.com/500. Are there any of these global and domestic leaders present in your city?
- For industry research within federal government agencies visit www.usejobs.gov. USAJobs is the US government's official website for listing civil service job openings. The site is sponsored by the United States Office of Personnel Management (OPM).
- When you are researching for local market leadership in the small businesses category, you may consider visiting the Better Business Bureau (BBB) at www.bbb.org. Although the BBB is not affiliated with federal, state, or local government, it could be a useful source to gather information on a business' reliability, as well as to alert you of any frauds committed against consumers by such. To become a BBB accredited business, the institution must meet and abide by certain standards of business practices. These standards should be added to the employer selection criteria set forth in the "hiring a mentor" approach. BBB Codes of Business practices can be found in the following link: www.bbb.org/us/ bbb-accreditation-standards/

What jobs do these top employers/market leaders need to fill? (Step 4)

To get an accurate answer, you are going to have to ask the employers themselves. They are the ones who really know what jobs need to get filled and what qualifications are required. In Step 4, you are going to research each employer recorded in Step 3's employer list. This is known as "inside research."

Employer inside research has three objectives. First is to find out what jobs are involved in an employer's daily operation; second, what their tasks are; and third, what their corresponding qualifications are. In this step, you and your parents are required to complete the Job List Activity, which captures all three of them. There are three examples on the next page for you to have an idea of what it could look like.

Employer: Brown & Brown Accounting Services

Column # 1 Job Position	Column # 2 Tasks	Column # 3 Qualifications (Education, Skills, and Experience)
Certified Public Accountant	• Complete income tax returns for individual clients and small businesses • Audit clients' financial records for IRS compliance • Create and analyze budgets • Recommend methods to save money • Increase client retention	**Education** • Bachelor Degree in Accounting • CPA Certified **Skills:** • Strong verbal and written communication skills • Attention to details • Customer service skills **Experience** Minimum of **1 year** of experience
Bookkeeper	• Monitor office supply levels and reorder as necessary • Pay vendor invoices • Issue invoices to customers • Collect sales taxes from customer sales and remit them to the government • Ensure that receivables are collected • Record cash receipts and make money deposits • Conduct a monthly reconciliation of bank accounts to ensure their accuracy • Maintain the petty cash fund • Maintain an accounting filing system • Maintain the annual budget • Calculate variances from the budget and report significant issues to leadership • Comply with local, state, and federal government reporting requirements • Process payroll • Provide clerical and administrative support	**Education** • QuickBooks® trained and certified • Coursework in accounting or business-related studies • High school diploma • Microsoft Office certified **Skills** • PC data entry and 10-key calculator skills • Knowledge of the bookkeeping/payroll software • Analytical and detail-oriented • Ability to work in a fast-paced team environment • Strong organizational and prioritizing skills • Strong verbal and written communication skills • Ability to work under strict deadlines, while organizing multiple projects at the same time • Knowledge of applicable local, state, and federal wage and hour laws **Experience:** • 2+ years of experience in bookkeeping services to include payroll, general ledgers, and financial statements
Client Services	• Greet incoming clients in a personalized and inviting manner • Schedule clients with a tax professional • Maintain clean and organized office	**Education** • High school diploma **Skills** • Strong customer service skills • Strong organizational and time-management skills • Knowledge of cash register operations • Knowledge and experience with Microsoft Office **Experience** No prior experience required

Employer: Smith & Company, P.A.

Job Position	Tasks	Education, Skills, and Experience (Qualifications)
Payroll Technician	• Enter, verify, and process employee time and attendance records using the time and attendance payroll system • Process employee data changes • Deliver instruction/training to employees regarding the use of payroll-related systems including clocking in and out, and online access of pay stub	**Education** • High school diploma • Related post-secondary coursework • Microsoft Office trained and certified – Excel knowledge at the advanced level **Skills** • Strong quantitative and analytical thinking skills • Attention to detail and thoroughness **Experience** • 2+ recent years of payroll processing experience

Job List Activity

Instruction: The goal of this activity is to list <u>all possible job positions/occupations</u> involved in the employer's daily operation. You don't have to repeat the same thing over and over if it has already been recorded. In the example above, Brown & Brown Accounting Services shows Certified Public Accountant, Bookkeeper, and Client Services; whereas for Smith & Company, P.A., only the Payroll Technician position was recorded. This is because, even though Smith & Company, P.A. was also looking for a bookkeeper and an accountant, we only documented the position we did not have. **When job positions start showing up over and over again and no new positions come out, stop and proceed to Step 5.**

To complete the Job List Activity, first start with the employer's official website. This information can be located in the contact information column of your Employer List. Once on the website, look for the Careers or Jobs tab. If available, subscribe to the employer's job alerts. This service sends you an email notification every time there is an opening. If there is no career tab on the website, your next option is online research. Chances are you may already have a good idea of all possible jobs from the activities in the previous steps (e.g., reading industry publications, job shadowing, informational interview, etc.). So, all you must do is search these jobs in search engines, such as www.monster.com or www.careerbuilder.com. Once in the job listing, you can find the rest of the information you need to fill out the tasks and qualifications column.

The last step is to conduct an informational interview with the individual you identified as your contact person in your Employer List. The purpose of the Informational Interview in Step 4 is to find out if there is any other additional information about qualifications that were not mentioned in the job posting but that are important to the employer. Sample questions for this activity include:

- What personality traits, special abilities, and skills fit best for this position?
- What makes some people successful at this job and others less so?
- What kind of attitude or qualities do they demonstrate?

These questions are designed to reveal what employers are really looking for in their candidates. The skills you commonly hear in informational interviews that are not always mentioned in job announcement posts include:

- **Accountability** (accepts responsibility for actions taken and keeps others informed of their outcomes)
- **Initiative** (identifies what needs to be done and acts without being asked)
- **Problem-Solving Skills/Critical thinking skills** (breaks down problems and considers all possible solutions)
- **Adaptability and Flexibility** (being open to change)
- **Teamwork** (promotes cooperation and commitment within a team to achieve goals)
- **Interpersonal Skills** (interacts well with others at work, to include the ability to deal with conflict effectively)

Record your findings in the qualification column.

To which of these <u>jobs</u> can I <u>contribute</u> the most? (Step 5)

Market leaders (top employers in a leading industry) are representative of what people want. The fact that they have capitalized on consumer demand effectively is what has earned them this role. Step 5 consists of identifying the skills these leaders need to fulfill the demand for their services/products. If market leaders are the vehicles that transport you to consumer demand, then you are left with the task of deciding how you plan to get on board. Let's begin explaining the significance of the two underlined words in the question posted on this step. *Jobs* refers to a group of tasks that employers need to cover to conduct business. The second word refers to an individual *contribution* to the employer's final product or service. Simply put, the objective of Step 5 is to figure out in which of the jobs listed in Step 4 you can be more useful to the employer. <u>The job you contribute to the most is the one where you can meet its educational requirements and where your natural skills can be put to the most productive use for the benefit of your employer's business operation.</u>

Having said this, direct your attention to the job list you created in Step 4 and take a closer look at column #3. Notice how a job qualification is made up of three components: Education, Skills, and Experience. Step 5 looks at the first two components: Education and Skills. To answer Step 5's question, you are going to perform <u>two sweeps</u> through Step 4's job list. In the first sweep, you are going to eliminate the job position that requires an education you are <u>not</u> willing to pursue. This is called the *Educational Path Decision*. Then, from the jobs that remain, you are going to identify the ones whose tasks <u>build upon</u> your unique skills and aptitudes. This final sweep is called the *Tasks-Skills Match*.

Have you ever heard the phrase "no pain, no gain"? Well, in this book we will use a similar phrase; it is called "no paper, no job." *Paper* refers to a degree, certification, or license that shows you have met the educational or vocational requirement for the job. For example, if the job opening specifically states that only candidates with a bachelor's degree in accounting will be considered, and you don't have that piece of paper that proves you have a bachelor's degree in accounting, you simply can't get the job. Therefore, as you look at each job's requirements, you are going to decide which position's educational path you are willing to commit to. There are four possible paths to decide from: the 4-year university path, the community college path, the vocational school path, and the apprenticeship path.

The 4-year university path: The 4-year university path is a bachelor degree program awarded by a university. These programs require 120 to 128 credits, although you can transfer up to 60 college credits from a community college. Bachelor's degrees consist of general education courses and electives in addition to the specific subject of study required courses, the "major." There are two types of bachelor's degrees; the Bachelor of Arts (BA) and the Bachelor of Science (BS). The BA requires you to take most of your courses in the liberal arts (e.g., language, literature, and humanities). The BS, on the other hand, requires you to take most of your courses in science (e.g., physics, chemistry, and mathematics).

The community college path: Community colleges are two-year schools that provide affordable post-secondary education as a pathway to a four-year degree. Most community colleges have what is called articulation of agreement. An articulation of agreement facilitates the transfer of college credits among state-assisted institutions so that students can continue to make progress toward their bachelor degree at a university. For example, some community colleges have agreements with their state universities that permit graduates of parallel programs to transfer with a junior standing. When considering this route, find out the credit transfer requirements of the university you want to attend. Also, some community colleges develop partnerships with local businesses to offer technical or vocational training tailored to their industries. Some of these training programs lead to job placement. This means that if this path is chosen, you could be fully trained for the workforce in an average of six months to a year. These programs are called professional certification programs. Examples include:

- Biotechnology: Biotechnology programs seek to prepare students for immediate entry-level employment in the biotechnology, pharmaceutical, or medical device manufacturing industry.
- Banking Specialist: These programs provide general knowledge and technical skills that establish a financial services career. The certificate includes career entry employees with clerical, administrative, or customer service tasks. Positions available under this program include customer service representative and financial/banking specialist. This program also meets the requirements for the Center for Financial Training national industry diploma.
- Accounting Technology Management: The Accounting Applications College Credit Certificate programs prepare students for employment as accounting clerks, data processing clerks, junior accountants, and assistant accountants, or to provide supplemental training for persons previously or currently employed in these occupations. The curriculum teaches students the principles, procedures, and theories of organizing and maintaining business and financial records, and the preparation of accompanying financial reports.
- Air Cargo Management: The Air Cargo Management College Credit Certificate program gives students the skills required to gain employment as an air cargo agent. These programs are usually completed in one or two semesters. Earned credits can be applied towards an Associate in Science degree in Aviation Administration.

The vocational school path: Vocational schools, also called trade schools, are post-secondary learning institutions that specialize in providing students with the technical skills they need to perform the tasks of a particular job within a certain industry. The duration of this program usually ranges from six months to a year. Examples of vocational schools include:

- Culinary schools
- Beauty and cosmetology schools
- Health care vocational schools that offer training for medical assistant technician, medical front office and billing, and patient care technician

The apprenticeship path: An apprenticeship is a program where the students learn a skilled trade through classroom work and on-the-job training at the same time. A student completing an apprenticeship program becomes a journeyperson (skilled craftsperson) in that trade. Most programs require a high school diploma or the completion of certain course work and/or may include other specific requirements, such as passing certain aptitude tests, proof of physical ability to perform the duties of the trade, and the possession of a valid driver's license. Since students are trained in the actual workplace and receive a salary, the program entrance process is like applying for a job. Apprenticeship programs prepare successful graduates to work as journeymen in the areas of electrical, fire sprinkler, air conditioning, refrigeration, heating, plumbing, sheet metal, and many other trades.

Educational Path Activity

Instructions: Add a fourth column to Step 4's job list as in the examples provided and name it Educational Path. Seek the assistance of an admission advisor or counselor from a local post-secondary school (e.g., college advisor or an admission representative). The information to be collected should include:

- Applicable post-secondary educational path
- Admission requirements for the post-secondary program (what it takes to get in, such as admission tests and GPA)
- Program's graduation requirements (what it takes to finish, such as duration of the program, amount of credits required, difficulty level, etc.)

The required educational path is usually listed in the actual job posting under qualifications (refer to examples). Otherwise, do some inside research on your own to find out the employer's desired education path for the job (e.g., bachelor, associate, certification, etc.). Once you have this information, contact a school advisor or counselor from the applicable post-secondary institution to gather the rest of the information, as in the example that follows.

Job Position: Registered Nurse

Tasks	Qualifications	Educational Path
• Administer medications to patients and monitor for side effects • Record medical information and vital signs • Consult and coordinate with team members to assess, plan, implement, or evaluate patient care plans	**Education** • Graduate of an accredited school of nursing • Bachelor of Science in Nursing (BSN) • Must be licensed in the state of Florida as a Registered Nurse (RN) **Skills** • Technical skills • Communication • Critical thinking • Interpersonal skills • Flexibility • Organizational skills • Professional accountability **Experience** One year of experience in a hospital setting	Bachelor of Science in Nursing (BSN) • Completion of a minimum of 43 credit hours • GPA of 3.60 in all attempted college course work • Maintain consistent advisement in the Department of Nursing for a minimum of one year prior to the application deadline • Pass Florida Registered Nurse (RN) Exam

After you get a good idea of what it takes to get in each of the programs and what it takes to graduate, go ahead and cross out the jobs with a path you are <u>not</u> willing to commit to. The jobs that remain will continue to the last sweep, the tasks–skills match activity.

Step 5 Helpers - High School Counselor and Teachers

As you can see, each job listed points to a specific educational path to be an eligible candidate (e.g., bachelor's degree, professional certifications, licenses, etc.). To assist you in making this decision, your **high school counselor and teachers** first asses your overall high school performance, then make recommendations as to the type, difficulty level, and duration of the academic program in which you are most likely to succeed (e.g., a 2-year vocational school curriculum versus a 4-year college curriculum).

However, this does <u>not</u> mean that because a student has failing grades in certain academic areas, he or she <u>should not consider</u> a 4-year university path. It simply means that this student will have to commit to work hard to bring his or her academic performance up to college level. Therefore, the issue to consider here is not how smart you are, but how hard you are willing to work. <u>It is about commitment and motivation, and has nothing to do with a student's potential or how smart he or she is.</u>

The question to ask at this point is: To which of these four educational paths am I <u>willing</u> to commit? This is something only you can answer. Remember what the Bible says: "For which of you, desiring to build a tower, does not first sit down and count the cost, whether he has enough to complete it?" (Luke 14:28 ESV).

Be honest with yourself, your parents, and your teachers. However, do not stress too much about this. When you make an educational path decision, you are not making a <u>permanent career decision</u> like you did in Step 2 when you decided what industry you were going to be part of. Here, you are just deciding what is going to be your initial educational path to meet the schooling requirement of your <u>first job</u> within the career that you have already chosen (how to get in the industry).

Can you change an occupation within an industry later and pursue further education within the field? Of course you can. Most likely you will anyway, whether you like it or not. There will be future industry changes outside your control that may force you to continue your education just for the sake of staying employed.

Tasks-Skills Match Activity

In this activity, you are going to focus on the <u>results or outcome</u> that your natural skills and personality type are most likely to produce. Employers look for candidates who have the potential of bringing a <u>benefit</u> to their organization (e.g., increase sales, bring improvement to service quality, etc.). Therefore, a good match between a task and an identified natural skill/personality type can positively affect an individual's results at a given task. Here is an example of how it works:

Outcome:
Generated 20
new accounts
versus 5 from the
previous quarter

Job Task: Deliver
product presentation
to group of clients

Natural Skill: verbal/linguistic abilities - Social Personality type

Notice how in this example, the individual's natural skill, combined with his or her personality type, formed the foundation for the result he or she was able to achieve (20 new accounts brought to the employer versus 5 on the previous presentation by another employee). In this same way, a well-defined base (a skill/natural ability, personality type, and job task match) can determine your contribution to the employer (e.g., solve a problem that nobody was able to find a solution for or bring an improvement to a product or service).

Given the importance of these underlying traits, identifying your natural skills and personality type combination is the <u>key factor</u> for a successful job match. A natural ability is a special facility for performing a certain task. The more accurately you can identify those natural abilities, the more effectively you can identify the jobs or occupations that build on those unique abilities.

Why is this task/natural ability match so important? The answer, again, is value. As mentioned earlier, employers look for candidates whose skills represent a gain to their business. In the example provided, the value is represented by the 20 new accounts this individual was able to bring on board because of his or her skills. A proper match between a natural ability, a personality type, and a skill, increases the chances for the kind of <u>results that an employer can benefit from</u>. This means that after you have identified an educational career path, ***the abilities that allow you to bring the greatest contribution to an employer within a leading industry is the career gift you have receive from God.***

To complete the Tasks-Skills Match Activity, you are going to have to work closely with a career coach. Under their guidance, you are going to determine which of the remaining jobs your natural abilities/personality type could have the most impact on. Traditionally, the job of career coaches has been to assess students' natural abilities, work environment preferences, personality, and values, to recommend a possible career fit. However, when finding out what students like to do, employers' needs are often ignored. To prevent this, the objective of career coaches is to identify and match your unique abilities and strengths to the employer's job tasks. Therefore, the question posted on this step is worded: To which of an employer's jobs can I contribute the most? This stresses the importance of moving from a self-centered approach (what I enjoy and makes me happy) to an employer value-based approach (how well I can do what the employer needs to be done).

Consider the following: "A wise man has great power…and a man of knowledge increases strength" (Proverbs 24:5 NKJV). A "wise man" has "great power" because he has taken the following actions:

- He or she has targeted the jobs in demand by a market leader, within a leading industry, with the resources to develop his or her skills and whose services match his or her career interest
- He or she has accounted for his or her natural skills by judging the outcomes of theses abilities in an actual work context (part-time job, internship, job shadowing, or voluntary work)
- He or she has tailored his or her education to the market leader's skills in demand to build upon his or her accounted natural abilities

"Knowledge" is information and self-awareness of one's received natural abilities/skills. The more accurately you define your unique abilities, the more effectively you can achieve a job task-natural skill match. Why is this task–skill correlation so important? Your natural skills determine the quality of the tasks you will be performing in your job, as the number of watts in a light bulb determine its brightness. Unless you have the natural abilities/skills that support the job tasks demands, you will not shine bright enough to be competitive. And *if you are not competitive, you don't have a career.*

The investor approach to career planning is founded on the simple fact that you are only responsible for developing what you have received, not for what you have not received. When the right job experience opportunity is presented (job shadowing, internship, or voluntary work), a natural skill is like cash money. You either have it, or you don't.

Besides the interest inventories you learned in step 2, career coaches utilize personality assessments and accomplishments exercises that can help you identify the unique abilities you possess and give you specific recommendations as to what jobs on the updated list would fit your profile.

Again, the objective of the career coach is to get to the very basics of your natural abilities and unique personality traits to match them to the tasks where they can be put to the most productive use. Once this is determined, you should be able to identify the job where you can bring the most benefit to the employer's business operation; *that* is your God-given career gift.

Step 5: Job Shadowing Activity

There are three pieces of information you need to give your career coach for them to help you in the Tasks–Skills Match Activity: your industry of interest, your updated job list (jobs that remained after the educational path activity), and a record of the occupational indicators you have observed. The first two pieces of information you should already have; therefore, the purpose of job shadowing in this step is to collect occupational indicators for your career coach to analyze.

During the first field exploration, the focus was on interest, and you were looking at the broad aspects of industries. In this activity, career exploration is narrowed down to the occupations listed on your updated job list, which means that this time, you are going to be paying close attention to the day-to-day tasks being performed by each job (use your employer list contacts from Step 3). As you conduct the job shadowing, ask yourself question such as:

- What tasks seem to come easy to you? For example, when given the opportunity during the job shadowing, you demonstrated a natural ability for handling certain precision tools with great accuracy.

- What tasks required a skill for which you have received praise from your teachers? For example, a job position requires oral presentation of a product to prospective clients, and you have repeatedly received praise from your speech teacher for your oral presentations in class.

- Was there any position that involved a task for which, when performed in other settings, you seemed to lose track of time and didn't want anyone or anything to disturb you? For example, a position that involved fixing engines, and in your free time you like to buy old cars and work on their engines.

- Was there any job that involved a task for which you, your friends, and/or family members have repeatedly said you are good at? For example, a job position that requires fixing computers, and friends/family members are always coming to you with issues with their computer.

Other Resources

You may take the Armed Services Vocational Aptitude Battery (ASVAB), sponsored by the Department of Defense, to help you identify interests, abilities, and personal preferences. This assessment consists of nine short tests covering word knowledge, paragraph comprehension, arithmetic reasoning, mathematics knowledge, general science, auto and shop information, mechanical comprehension, electronics information, and assembling objects. Scores are provided on a report called the ASVAB Student Result Sheet (usually within thirty days), together with a copy of *The ASVAB Workbook*, which explains ASVAB results and how to match the student's profile to 250 civilian and military occupations. Since composite scores measure the student's aptitude/capacity for handling more advanced academic training, a certain amount of preparation is required to achieve the best possible results. Achieving a maximum score increases vocational opportunities, as the armed forces use the ASVAB results to determine not only the individual's qualifications for enlistment, but also for determining the types of jobs and training for which the person is best suited. The ASVAB can be taken any time after the tenth grade and scores are good for two years; however, sophomore scores are not accepted for enlistment. **Taking the ASVAB does not obligate a student to join the military.**

Notes

Conclusion

In conclusion, these five steps will lead you to discover the gifts God bestowed in your life, as promised. But if you need detailed instructions on how to choose a specific school for your post-secondary education and how to secure your first job after graduation with a targeted employer, then you need to obtain of a copy of *Career Planning for High School Students* starting in step 6.

For now, let's review the key points of the investor approach to career discovery and planning.

- ✓ Identify leading industries where you live (Step 1)
- ✓ Identify the industry of interest (Step 2)
- ✓ Identify the top employer (market leader) of this industry (Step 3)
- ✓ Identify the jobs that this top employer needs to fill (Step 4)
- ✓ Identify the job to which you can contribute the most (Step 5)

By following these simple steps, you will ensure that you have identified the gift you have received, and know how to exploit it to achieve the highest return on God's investment, just as a good steward would do. That is, one last time, ***the abilities that allow you to bring the greatest contribution to a market leader within a leading industry is the career gift you have received from God.***

The Ultimate Career Goal

The goal of the prerequisites and investor approach to career planning is to secure an everlasting career reward. Jesus says: "And, behold, I come quickly; and my reward is with me, to give every man according as his work shall be" (Revelation 22:12 KJV). Therefore: "Labour not for the meat which perisheth, but for that meat which endureth unto everlasting life, which the Son of man shall give unto you: for him hath God the Father sealed" (John 6:27).

The gospel mission is the destination of your career gift after having been developed by a market leader within a leading industry sector, as established in the investor approach to career planning and discovery presented in this book. This is how an everlasting career reward is secured. Your mission in life, as one who has trusted Christ as Savior, is to serve Jesus, and good service is marked by good stewardship of the career ability God has given you.

One of history's most popular examples of this biblical truth was Solomon. King Solomon received the task to build the first temple to God (a more recent version of the tabernacle). Considering the fact that the new king could lead his beloved Israel to a closer relationship with Him, God granted Solomon the opportunity to ask for whatever he wanted. Solomon, per the motivation of his heart, did not ask for riches and glory. Instead, he asked for wisdom to act upon God's mission (draw sinners to have a relationship with Him, in this case, through the temple), so Solomon received the wisdom he requested (just like Oholiab and Bezalel). With the gift of wisdom, Solomon judged Israel, built the first temple, and still got to keep it for personal use as well, obtaining riches and glory for himself as a consequence.

You must comprehend that God does give gifts to men if they purpose in their heart to fulfill His mission. This book is nothing but a recruiting tool intended to prompt you to tailor your career plan to exploit God's only weakness, namely his uncontrollable passion for the lost souls. God himself calls you to do this in his own words: "Then saith he unto his disciple, The harvest truly is plenteous, but the labourers are few; Pray ye therefore the Lord of the harvest, that he will send forth labourers into his harvest" (Matthew 9:37-38).

The primitive church was a church of labourers, who understood very well this truth. The following verses give us a picture of what this church looked like: "All the believers were together and had everything in common. Selling their possessions and goods, they gave to anyone as he had need. Every day they continued to meet in the temple courts. They broke bread in their homes and ate together with glad and sincere hearts, praising God and enjoying the favor of the people. And the Lord added to their number daily those who were being saved" (Acts 2:44-47 NKJV).

There is a direct relation between the career efforts of God's workers and the number of souls that are being saved. Therefore, you can obtain a greater everlasting career reward by increasing your impact to the gospel mission through your local church. This is done by targeting the market leaders within a leading industry with the resources to guarantee you a greater return for your skills. This is simply called good stewardship.

In this book, the secret of receiving God's career gift has been revealed to you. However, the decision to act upon this truth and receive the ultimate everlasting career reward lies with you. If you want to take this opportunity, go ahead and return to step 1 of the investor approach to career planning and discovery and let's get started. The decision is yours.